Student Interactive

myView
LITERACY

K

SAVVAS
LEARNING COMPANY

ISBN-13: 978-0-134-90873-1

ISBN-10: 0-134-90873-2

7 2021

Julie Coiro, Ph.D.

Jim Cummins, Ph.D.

Pat Cunningham, Ph.D.

Elfrieda Hiebert, Ph.D.

Pamela Mason, Ed.D.

Ernest Morrell, Ph.D.

P. David Pearson, Ph.D.

Frank Serafini, Ph.D.

Alfred Tatum, Ph.D.

Sharon Vaughn, Ph.D.

Judy Wallis, Ed.D.

Lee Wright, Ed.D.

Then and Now

WEEK 1

Genre | Narrative Nonfiction

READING WORKSHOP
Infographic: Making Communication Better

FOUNDATIONAL SKILLS Short o and Long o **16**

 *Cars Are Always Changing* .... Narrative Nonfiction **31**
by Gary Miller

Reading Comprehension • Describe Connections

READING-WRITING BRIDGE **45**

Academic Vocabulary • Spell Words • Read Like a Writer, Write for a Reader •
Language and Conventions: Complete Sentences

WRITING WORKSHOP **49**

Plan Your Personal Narrative

WEEK 2

Genre | Narrative Nonfiction

READING WORKSHOP
Infographic: Learning About the Past

FOUNDATIONAL SKILLS Short u and Long u **54**

 *Uncovering the Past* .... Narrative Nonfiction **69**
by Jennifer Torres

Reading Comprehension • Find Main Idea and Supporting Details

READING-WRITING BRIDGE **83**

Academic Vocabulary • Spell Words • Read Like a Writer, Write for a Reader •
Language and Conventions: Kinds of Sentences

WRITING WORKSHOP **87**

Write Your Personal Narrative

WEEK 3

Genre | Fiction

READING WORKSHOP
Time Line: Changing Phones

FOUNDATIONAL SKILLS Short e and Long e 92

Grandma's Phone .... Fiction 107
by Ken Mochizuki

Reading Comprehension • Describe Setting

READING-WRITING BRIDGE 121

Academic Vocabulary • Spell Words • Read Like a Writer, Write for a Reader •
Language and Conventions: End Punctuation

WRITING WORKSHOP 125

Organize Your Personal Narrative

WEEK 4

Genre | Narrative Nonfiction

READING WORKSHOP
Infographic: Then and Now

FOUNDATIONAL SKILLS Review and Reinforce: Words for Pp, Yy, Short i, Long i 130

***Changing Laws, Changing Lives:
Martin Luther King, Jr.*** .... Narrative Nonfiction 143
by Eric Velasquez

Reading Comprehension • Find Text Features

READING-WRITING BRIDGE 157

Academic Vocabulary • Spell Words • Read Like a Writer, Write for a Reader •
Language and Conventions: Question Words

WRITING WORKSHOP 161

Edit Your Personal Narrative

WEEK 5

Genre | Fiction

READING WORKSHOP
Poem: A Family Tradition

FOUNDATIONAL SKILLS Review and Reinforce: Words for Dd, Ff, Vv, Short e 166

Tempura, Tempera .... Fiction 179
by Lyn Miller-Lachmann

Reading Comprehension • Determine Theme

READING-WRITING BRIDGE 193

Academic Vocabulary • Spell Words • Read Like a Writer, Write for a Reader •
Language and Conventions: Question Words

WRITING WORKSHOP 197

Share Your Personal Narrative

WEEK 6

Infographic: Compare Across Texts

FOUNDATIONAL SKILLS Review and Reinforce: Words for Hh, Xx, Short u, Long u 202

PROJECT-BASED INQUIRY 212

Inquire: Looking Back • **Collaborate and Discuss:** Informational Text • **Conduct Research:**
Conduct an Interview • **Celebrate and Reflect**

REFLECT ON THE UNIT 219

Then and Now

Essential Question

What can we learn from the past?

▶ **Watch**

"**Changing Technology**" and see what you can learn about how technology changes.

SAVVAS realize™
Go ONLINE for all lessons.

 VIDEO

 AUDIO

 GAME

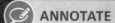 ANNOTATE

 BOOK

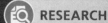 RESEARCH

TURN and TALK

What technology do you use?

Reading Workshop

Infographic: Making Communication Better
Cars Are Always Changing .... **Narrative Nonfiction**
by Gary Miller

Infographic: Learning About the Past
Uncovering the Past .... **Narrative Nonfiction**
by Jennifer Torres

Time Line: Changing Phones
Grandma's Phone .... **Fiction**
by Ken Mochizuki

Infographic: Then and Now
Changing Laws, Changing Lives:
Martin Luther King, Jr. .... **Narrative Nonfiction**
by Eric Velasquez

Poem: A Family Tradition
Tempura, Tempera .... **Fiction**
by Lyn Miller-Lachmann

Reading-Writing Bridge

• Academic Vocabulary • Spelling • Read Like a Writer,
Write for a Reader • Language and Conventions

Writing Workshop

• Plan Your Personal Narrative • Compose Plot • What Happens Last **Personal Narrative**
• Edit for Subjective and Possessive Pronouns • Publish and Celebrate

Project-Based Inquiry

• Inquire • Research • Collaborate

Read Together

Independent Reading

Ask questions to make connections when you read.

1. How is the text like other texts I have read?

2. How does the text remind me of my life?

3. How does the text remind me of my community?

Directions Read the information to students. Say: When you make connections, you think about how the text you are reading is like another text or real life. As students read texts independently, encourage them to make connections to other texts, to personal experiences, and to society.

My Independent Reading Log

Date	Book	Pages Read	My Ratings
			☺ ☺ ☹
			☺ ☺ ☹
			☺ ☺ ☹
			☺ ☺ ☹

Directions Have students self-select a text and interact independently with it for increasing periods of time. To build stamina, tell students to read a few more pages every day. Then have them tell about their independent reading by completing the chart.

11

Unit Goals

In this unit, you will

○ read narrative nonfiction

△ write a personal narrative

☐ talk about what we can learn from the past

TURN and TALK Talk about how the classrooms are alike and different.

Directions Read aloud the unit goals. Then have students look at the pictures. Ask them to talk about how the classroom from the past and the classroom today are alike and different.

Academic Vocabulary

time	
change	
discover	
tradition	

 **TURN and TALK** Say the words and act them out.

Directions Read the Academic Vocabulary to students and have them discuss the meanings of the words using the pictures. Then have partners take turns saying a vocabulary word for the other partner to act out.

Making Communication Better

Long ago people used a quill to write messages.

They dipped the quill in ink.

Then they wrote the message on paper.

14

Weekly Question

Why is it important to make inventions better?

Today we can use computers to write messages.

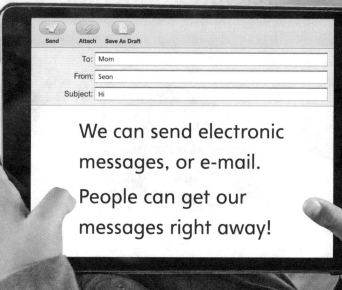

Send Attach Save As Draft

To: Mom

From: Sean

Subject: Hi

We can send electronic messages, or e-mail.

People can get our messages right away!

 **MY TURN** (Circle)

Directions Read the text as students look at the pictures. Explain that a digital text is a text we read on a screen, such as a computer or tablet. Have them recognize and discuss characteristics of an e-mail, such as the subject line. Then ask students to circle the parts of an e-mail in the picture.

Middle Sounds

 **SEE** *and* **SAY** (Circle) and <u>underline</u>

  STOP

Directions Have students name the pictures in each pair. Say: Circle the picture word that has the /o/ sound in the middle. Underline the picture word that has the /ō/ sound in the middle.

Short o and Long o

 **MY TURN** (Circle)

r o d

r o d e

Directions Tell students that the letter o can make the sound /o/ and the vowel pattern o_e can make the sound /ō/. **Say:** You will see the letter o in many words that have the short or long o sound. Trace the letter in the first word and tell me the sound that o makes in the word. Now circle the picture words in the first row that have the same o sound in the middle. **Continue** with the second row and the long o sound.

Short o and Long o

 Read and write

t o p

d o t

r o p e

Directions Have students name each picture and trace the letter or letters in the word. Then have them read each word and write it on the lines.

Sounds

 Circle

Directions Model: Listen to the sounds in this word: /b/ /o/ /ks/, *box*. The middle sound in *box* is /o/. Have students segment and blend the sounds in the picture words in the first row. Ask them to circle the ones that have the sound /o/. Continue with the second row and the sound /ō/.

19

Short o and Long o

 Color

f o x   h o m e

Directions Review the long and short o sounds with students. Have them trace the letters and say the vowel sound in each word. Then have students identify the vowel sound in each picture word. Say: If the vowel sound is /o/ like in *fox*, color the circle red. If the vowel sound is /ō/ like in *home*, color the circle blue.

My Words to Know

find	over	again

My Sentences to Read

 **MY TURN**

He can look <u>over</u> here.

He is going to look again.

Will he find her?

_____

- -

_____

Directions Have students read the high-frequency words and underline the words in the sentences. Then have them read the sentences. Say: Now you will write one of the words on the lines. Form each letter correctly as you write the word.

Short o and Long o

 **MY TURN** Read

 h o t

 l o g

 b o x

 m o m

 p o l e

 n o t e

22

Directions Remind students that the letter o can make the short o sound and the vowel pattern o_e can make the long o sound. Have students name the pictures and trace the letter or letters in each word. Then have them read the words.

On the Run

Highlight the words with the long **o** sound.

Dot broke her rope.

But we will find her.

We got GPS in her tag.

 AUDIO
Audio with Highlighting

 ANNOTATE

23

Look! It is her tag.

Can we get GPS in Dot?

24

Underline the words with the short **o** sound.

Mom, she is over here!

Do not do that again, Dot.

Short o and Long o

 Underline and read

 p<u>o</u>p **top** **stop**

 fox **box** **ox**

 hole **role** **pole**

 joke **poke** **woke**

26

Directions Review the sounds for short and long o. Then say: We can make new words by changing, adding, or taking away a letter. Have students look at each row of words and underline the letters that are the same in all three words. Ask them to identify the letter that was changed, added, or deleted. Then have students take turns reading the words with a partner.

Short o and Long o

 Circle and underline

The dog had a bone.

Ron is at the pond.

Bob can dig a hole.

Jill rode her bike.

Directions Have students read the sentences. Ask them to circle words with the short o sound and underline words with the long o sound.

Read Together

My Learning Goal

I can read narrative nonfiction.

SPOTLIGHT ON GENRE

Narrative Nonfiction

Narrative nonfiction tells a story about real people, places, and events.

Real People • Neil Armstrong was an astronaut.

Real Places • He went to the moon.

Real Events • The rocket ship landed. Neil took a step. He was the first person on the moon!

TURN and TALK Talk about how you know this is narrative nonfiction.

28

Directions Read aloud the genre information. Say: Narrative nonfiction can have characters, a setting, and main events, just like a story. Read the model text and have students talk about how they know it is narrative nonfiction.

Narrative Nonfiction

Anchor Chart

We can tell how the people, places, events, or ideas we read about are alike and different.

Cars Are Always Changing

Preview Vocabulary

crank

radio

engine

CD player

Read

Read the text and look at the pictures to learn about how cars have changed.

Meet the Author

Gary Miller loves to hike, kayak, and fish. When he is not exploring the outdoors, you will probably find him reading a mystery novel or playing his guitar.

30

Cars Are Always Changing

written by Gary Miller

🔊 **AUDIO**

Audio with Highlighting

✏ **ANNOTATE**

My mother took me to the car museum.
I learned a lot about cars.
They are always changing.

CLOSE READ

How did the first cars start? Underline the words that tell the answer.

The first cars did not start with a key. Instead, you turned a crank.

This car was made in 1913.
Its engine was small.
It could not go very fast.

CLOSE READ

How did the next cars start? Underline the words that tell the answer.

The next cars started with a key.
This car is from 1921.
It had a big engine. It could go fast!

Every year, car makers invented new parts. The parts made cars better and more fun.

CLOSE READ

How did cars change? Highlight the most important information.

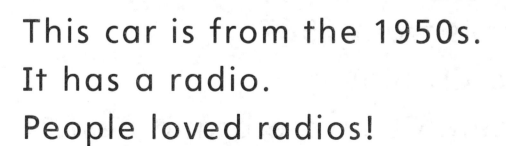

This car is from the 1950s.

It has a radio.

People loved radios!

This car is from 1987.

It has a CD player.

Back then, CDs were brand new!

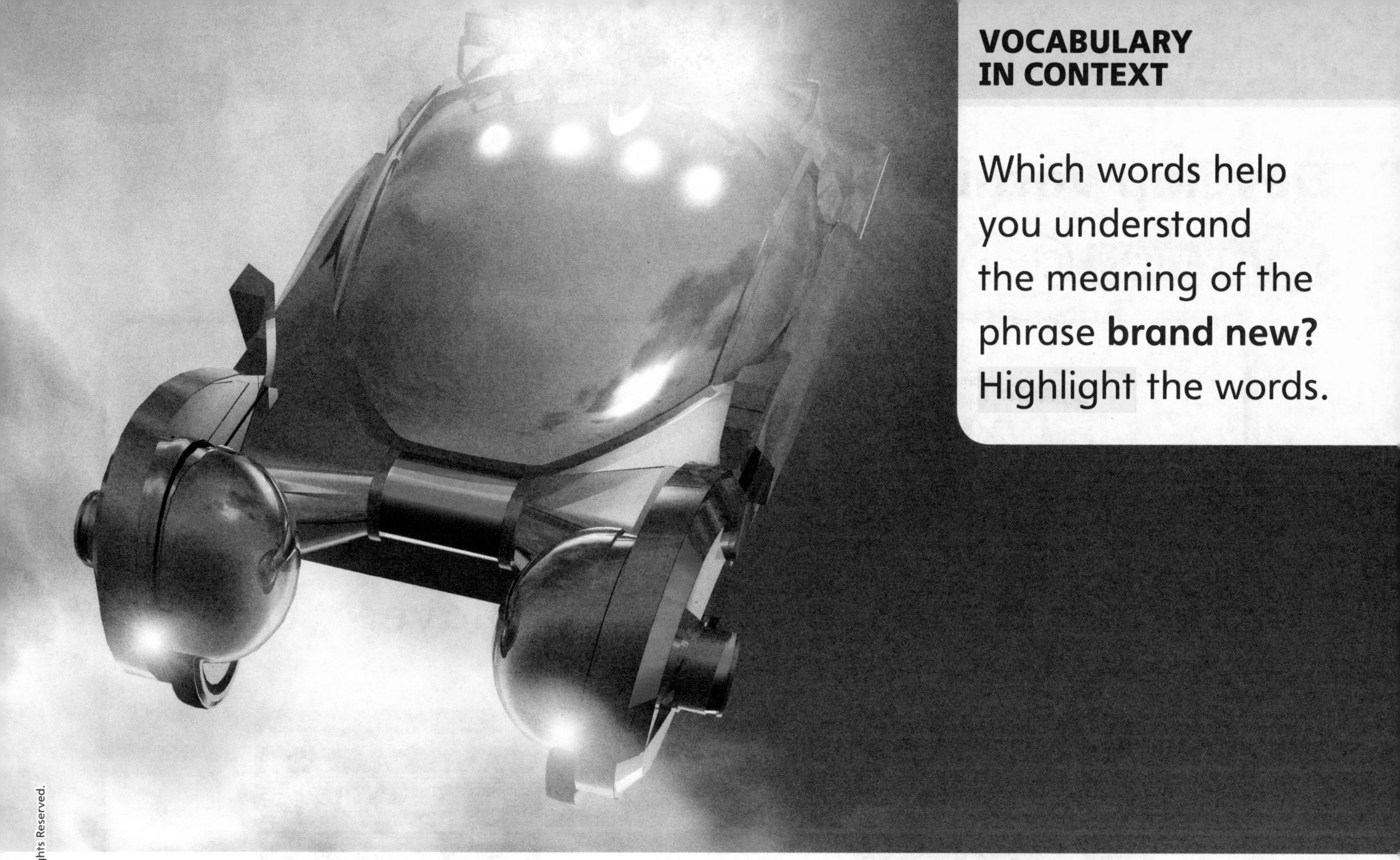

VOCABULARY IN CONTEXT

Which words help you understand the meaning of the phrase **brand new?** Highlight the words.

Cars are always changing.
Now we have cars that drive themselves.
Maybe future cars will fly!

39

Read Together

Develop Vocabulary

 MY TURN (Circle)

(engine) radio

CD player   crank

engine   CD player

radio   crank

Directions Read the words below each picture to students. Have them circle the word that names the picture.

Check for Understanding

 MY TURN Write

1. How is this text like a story?

_____

_____

_____

2. How does the author tell facts about cars?

_____

_____

_____

3. How do cars change over time?

_____

_____

_____

Directions Read the questions to students and have them write their responses on the lines. Remind them to use text evidence.

Describe Connections

Authors can connect information in a text.

They can tell how objects or events are alike and different.

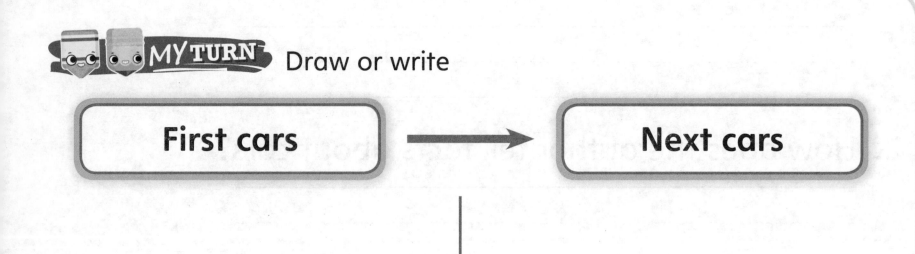

MY TURN Draw or write

| First cars | → | Next cars |

Directions Read the information to students. Ask them to describe connections in the text by drawing or writing details about the first cars in the first column and details about ways the next cars changed, or were different, in the second column. Remind students to look back at what they underlined in the text.

Find Important Details

Details tell more about a topic.

 Draw

Directions Read the information to students. Say: Finding the most important details in a text will help you better understand what you are reading. Have students evaluate details about cars in the text and draw two important details in the boxes. Remind them to look back at what they highlighted.

Reflect and Share

 TURN and TALK What happens at the car museum? What is another text you have read about a trip to a special place? Tell about each text.

At the car museum...

At the art store...

Weekly Question

Why is it important to make inventions better?

Directions Tell students they read about a trip to a car museum. Ask them to think of another text they read that tells about a trip to a special place. Then have students respond to sources by retelling the texts. Remind them that when they retell a text, they tell the most important ideas and details.

44

Read Together

I can use words to tell about narrative nonfiction.

My Learning Goal

Academic Vocabulary

| time | change | discover | tradition |

MY TURN Write

_____

Ali _____ a new park in her neighborhood.

| discovered | discovery |

Directions Read aloud the sentence and the answer choices. Review the meaning of *discover* with students and discuss the meanings of the related words *discovered* and *discovery*. Then have students write the word that best completes the sentence on the lines.

Spell Words

 **MY TURN** Sort and spell

hop	box	mop
find	dot	over

hop

Directions Say: Short *o* is often spelled *o* in words with three letters. Some words do not follow a pattern, so you have to remember how to spell them. Have students determine if each word follows the CVC pattern. Then have them spell and write the CVC words in the left column and the high-frequency words in the right column.

Read Like a Writer, Write for a Reader

 Write

1. Find words in the text that help you know who tells the story.

   _____

   _____

2. Write a sentence as the narrator. Tell what you see at the museum.

   _____

   _____

Directions Tell students that sometimes a character is the narrator of a text. Say: When a character is the narrator, the author uses words such as *I* and *we*. Have students listen to and experience first-person text as you read aloud a page from the text. Then read the items and have students write their responses.

Read Together

Complete Sentences

A **complete sentence** has a naming part and an action part.

A sentence begins with a capital letter.

<u>The woman</u> drives the car.

TURN and TALK Talk about the parts of the sentence.

MY TURN Circle and write

_____

the girls _____.

48

Directions Read aloud the information. Have partners identify the naming part and action part of the model sentence. Then read the sentence part at the bottom of the page. Ask students to edit the sentence by circling the letter that should be capitalized and writing a word or phrase to form a complete sentence.

My Learning Goal

I can write a story about myself.

Personal Narrative

A **personal narrative** is a true story about an event in the writer's life.

The writer uses words such as **I** and **me.**

People →• <u>Dad and I</u> went

Setting →• to <u>the zoo</u> last week.

First, we saw lions. ————— Plot

Next, we saw monkeys.

Last, we saw penguins.

Directions Say: When you read in English, you read from left to right. When you get to the end of a line, move your finger down to the beginning of the next line. Have students track the print as you read aloud the model text. Discuss the people in the text with students and identify the author as the narrator.

Generate Ideas

 Draw

| Possible event | → | Possible event |

50

Directions Say: Authors think of ideas before they write. When authors plan a personal narrative, they think about real events in their life they can tell a story about. Ask students to generate ideas for a class narrative as you draw the ideas on the board. Then have students generate ideas for their personal narrative by drawing events they might tell about in the graphic organizer.

Plan Your Personal Narrative

Authors organize their ideas before they write.

People

Setting

Event

 **TURN and TALK** Talk about your personal narrative.

Directions Say: One way authors organize their ideas is by talking about the people, setting, and event before they write. Have students organize their ideas orally by talking with a partner about their personal narrative, including the people, setting, and event they will write about.

Learning About the Past

We can learn about the past in different ways.

We can read about the past.

Weekly Question

How do we learn about the past?

We can hear about what the past was like.

We can study objects from the past.

TURN and TALK Talk about ways you can learn about the past.

Directions Read the text and have students look at the pictures. Ask them to describe personal connections by talking with a partner about how they can learn about the past.

Middle Sounds

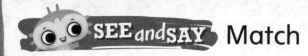 SEE and SAY Match

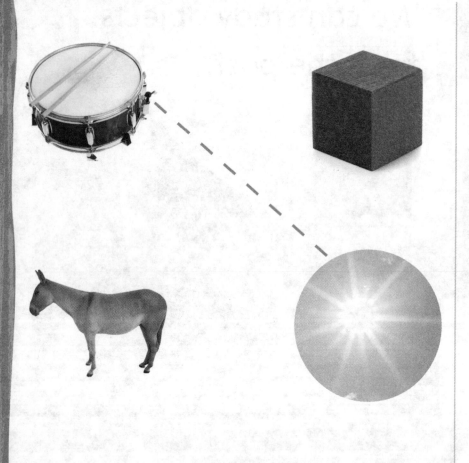

Directions Review the long and short *u* sounds with students. Have students name each picture word in the first set and identify the middle sound. Then have them draw lines to match the picture words with the same middle sounds. Continue with the second set of pictures.

Short u and Long u

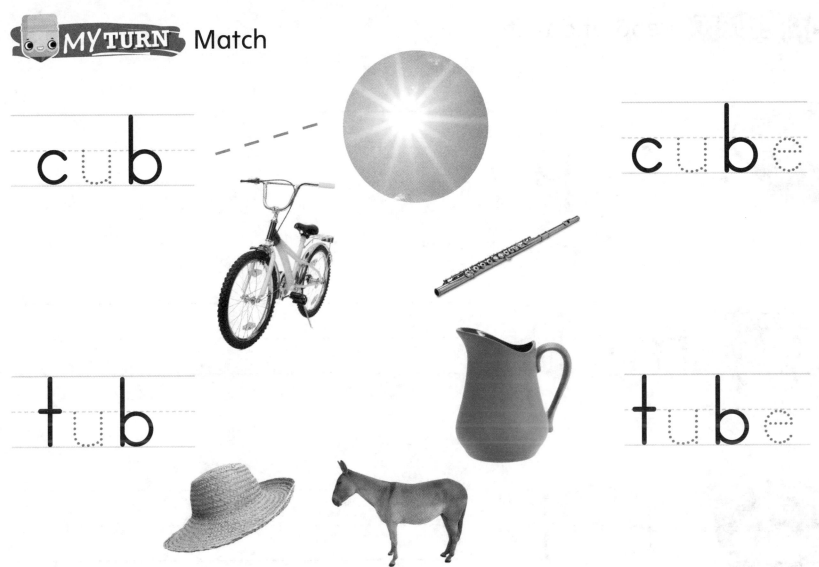

MY TURN Match

c u b

c u b e

t u b

t u b e

Directions Say: The letter *u* can make the sound /u/. The vowel pattern *u_e* can make the sound /ū/. You will see the letter *u* in many words that have the short or long *u* sound. Have students trace the letter or letters in each word and say the vowel sound. Then have them draw a line from each word to a picture word that has the same vowel sound in the middle.

Short u and Long u

 Read and write

 c u p

 m u l e

 h u t

Directions Have students name the picture and trace the letter or letters in each word. Then have them read the words. Finally, ask students to write the words on the lines.

Identify Words

 **SEE** and **SAY** (Circle,) clap, and count

Directions Have students name the images in the picture and circle the picture words with the middle sound /u/ or /ū/. Then say sentences about the picture. Have students identify the individual words in each sentence by clapping for each word they hear and counting the words.

Short u and Long u

 Underline

 cut

 cute

Directions Remind students that the letter *u* can make the short *u* sound and the vowel pattern *u_e* can make the long *u* sound. Have students trace the letter in the first word and identify the sound for *u*. Then have them underline the picture words in the first row that have the same vowel sound. Continue with the second row and the long *u* sound.

My Words to Know

all	now	pretty

My Sentences to Read

We all have a hat.

The red one is pretty.

Now we can go in the sun.

Directions Say: There are some words that we have to remember and practice, such as *now*. Have students read the high-frequency words. Then have them read the sentences and underline the high-frequency words in the sentences.

Short u and Long u

 **MY TURN** Read and write

cub	rule
bus	June
mug	cute

- -

- -

Directions Remind students that the letter *u* can make the sound /u/ and the vowel pattern *u_e* can make the sound /ū/. Have students read the words and identify the vowel sound in each word. Then have them write or dictate a sentence using at least one of the words.

Highlight the words with the long **u** sound.

A Look at the Past

He said, "A mule can help us."

The mule is big.

He said, "I made a tin cup."

The cup is cute.

AUDIO

Audio with Highlighting

ANNOTATE

She said, "I made a rag r<u>u</u>g."

The rug is pretty.

Underline the words with the short **u** sound.

She said, "I bake all the time.

Now we can have a hot bun."

Yum!

Short u and Long u

 **Read**

cube   sun   rug   tune

cup   cute   mule   mud

 **Draw**

64

Directions Remind students that the letter *u* can make the sound /u/ and the vowel pattern *u_e* can make the sound /ū/. Have students take turns reading the words with a partner. Then have them draw a picture to illustrate one of the words they read.

Short u and Long u

 Read and write

| tub | fun | tune | cube |

1. The game is ___fun___.

2. A _____ is in the cup.

3. The pup is in the _____.

Directions Review the sounds for short and long *u* with students. Have them read the words in the word bank. Then have them read the sentences. Ask students to write a word from the word bank on the lines to complete each sentence.

Read Together

My Learning Goal I can read narrative nonfiction.

SPOTLIGHT ON GENRE

Narrative Nonfiction

Narrative nonfiction tells facts about the real world.

- Neil Armstrong went to the moon.
- He got rocks from the moon.

TURN and TALK Do the sentences tell facts? How do you know? Talk to your partner.

Directions Remind students that narrative nonfiction tells a story about real people, places, and events. Say: Narrative nonfiction tells facts about the people, places, and events. A fact is information that can be proved to be true. Have partners discuss how they know the statements are facts.

Narrative Nonfiction
Anchor Chart
Main Idea

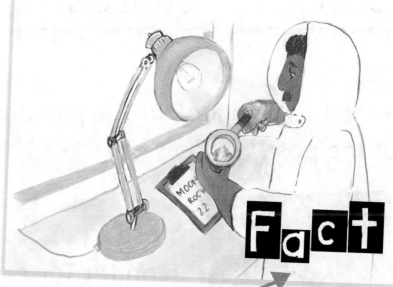

Neil Armstrong helped us learn about the moon.

Uncovering the Past
Preview Vocabulary

past

shovels

brushes

scientists

Read

Read the text and look at the pictures to find out how we can learn about the past.

Meet the Author

Jennifer Torres works as a newspaper reporter, writing stories that tell us about our world and about ourselves. She also writes books for children.

Uncovering the Past

written by Jennifer Torres

illustrated by Lisa Fields

 AUDIO

Audio with Highlighting

 ANNOTATE

One day in Mexico, workers were digging.
They were near a hill.

70

CLOSE READ

How did workers feel when they hit a stone? Highlight the words that help you answer the question.

Oh, no! They hit stone that did not move. They stopped digging.

71

The stone was pink. It looked very old.
Scientists came to see it.

CLOSE READ

Why do you think the scientists read books? Highlight the words that help you answer the question.

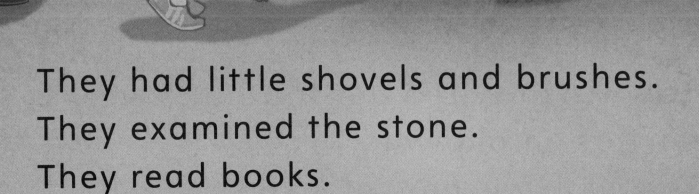

They had little shovels and brushes.
They examined the stone.
They read books.

Scientists figured out the stone was
part of an old wall.
The wall was part of a sports arena.

VOCABULARY IN CONTEXT

What does the word **arena** mean? Highlight the words that help you.

Long ago people played games in the arena.
They used a black rubber ball.

75

The scientists were excited!
They uncovered more of the arena.

CLOSE READ

What is the main idea of the text? Underline the sentence that tells the main idea.

Studying old things
can teach us about the past.

Develop Vocabulary

 Match

shovels

brushes

past

scientists

Directions Read the words to students. Then have them draw a line from each word to the matching picture.

Check for Understanding

 **MY TURN** (Circle) and write

1. Who is the text mostly about?

students	scientists

2. How do pictures help the author tell the story?

_____

- -

_____

3. Why were scientists excited about the wall?

_____

- -

_____

Directions Read question 1 and the answer choices aloud to students. Have them circle the answer. Then read questions 2 and 3 aloud and have students write their responses. Remind them to use text evidence.

Find Main Idea and Supporting Details

The **central**, or **main, idea** is what the text is mostly about.

Supporting evidence, or details, tells more about the main idea.

 Write and circle

_____

- -

_____

Directions Read the information aloud and have students look back at what they underlined in the text. Ask them to write the main idea of the text in their own words. Then have students circle the picture that supports the main idea.

Make Inferences

 **MY TURN** Draw and write

_____

- -

_____

_____

- -

_____

_____

- -

_____

_____

- -

_____

Directions Remind students that they can use details in the text and what they already know to make inferences. Ask: How do the workers feel when they hit stone? Why do the scientists read books? Have students draw the answer to each question and write evidence from the text that supports their understanding. Remind students to look back at what they highlighted.

Reflect and Share

MY TURN Write

_____

- -

_____

- -

_____

- -

_____

- -

_____

Weekly Question

How do we learn about the past?

Directions Say: You can respond to a text by writing about what you have learned. Have students write one thing they learned about the past from this text and one thing they learned about the past from another text they have read.

Read Together

I can use words to tell about narrative nonfiction.

My Learning Goal

Academic Vocabulary

time	change	discover	tradition

 Match

tradition

find

discover

custom

Directions Read the words and have students draw a line to match each word on the left to the word on the right that has a similar meaning.

Spell Words

 **MY TURN** Sort and spell

all	but	fun
rug	cup	now

but

Directions Say: Short *u* is often spelled *u* in words with three letters. Some words do not follow a pattern, so you have to remember how to spell them. Have students determine if each word follows the CVC pattern. Then have them spell and write the CVC words in the left column and the high-frequency words in the right column.

Read Like a Writer, Write for a Reader

 Write

1. What words does the author use to help you picture the ball?

_____

_____

2. Imagine you are the author. What word could you use to help readers picture the arena?

_____

_____

Directions Remind students that authors use words that help readers visualize, or picture in their minds, what is happening. Read the items one at a time and have students write their responses. Remind them to look back at the text.

Kinds of Sentences

Telling sentences tell something.

Asking sentences ask a question.

Exclamations show strong feelings.

They play a game. Is the ball black? They win!

 **MY TURN** (Circle) and write

____

we play baseball ____

Directions Say: All sentences begin with a capital letter. Telling sentences end with a period. Asking sentences end with a question mark. Exclamations end with an exclamation point. **Read the sentence at the bottom of the page. Have students edit the sentence by circling the letter that should be capitalized and writing the correct punctuation mark at the end.**

I can write a story about myself.

Compose Setting

The **setting** is where and when a narrative takes place.

 Circle

Directions Say: In a personal narrative, the setting is a real place that you have been to at a real time. Have students tell what they see in each picture. Have them circle the pictures that show a setting they could tell about in a personal narrative. Direct students to dictate or compose the setting for their personal narrative.

Narrator

The **narrator** is the person who is telling the story.

The narrator tells about the people, setting, and events.

 **MY TURN** Cross out and draw

Directions Say: The narrator in a personal narrative is usually the author. Have students look at the people in the pictures and identify which one could be in a narrative about themselves. Have them draw an X over the person who could not. Then have students draw a picture of another person they might tell about in a narrative about themselves.

Compose Plot

The **plot** is the main events in a narrative.

Events can tell about a problem and a resolution.

 Draw

Directions Remind students that a problem is something in a narrative that needs to be fixed and the resolution is how the problem is fixed. Ask students to explain the problem shown in the picture. Then have them compose the plot by drawing a resolution to the problem. Direct students to dictate or compose the plot for their personal narrative.

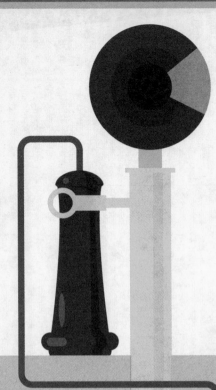

Changing Phones

Inventions change our lives.

New phones make it easier to communicate.

Past

This is one of the first phones. There were no numbers! Operators helped people make phone calls.

Weekly Question

How has communication changed over time?

This is a phone today.
People make calls on smartphones.
People do other things on their phones too!

Present

TURN and **TALK** What questions do you have about phones?

Directions Tell students that sometimes we want to learn more about interesting topics, so we ask questions for informal inquiry. Read the information on the time line and have students look at the pictures. Ask them to discuss the questions they have.

Middle Sounds

 Circle

Directions Say: Listen as I say the sounds in the word *bed*: /b/ /e/ /d/. The middle sound is /e/. Now listen as I say the sounds in the word *bead*: /b/ /ē/ /d/. The middle sound is /ē/. Have students name each picture then circle the picture words in each row that have the same middle vowel sound.

Short e and Long e

 Say and match

J e n

E v e

P e t e

T e d

Directions Say: The letter e can make the sound /e/. The vowel pattern e_e can make the sound /ē/. You will see the letter e in many words that have the long or short e sound. Have students trace the letter or letters in each word and say the vowel sound. Then have them draw lines to match the words with the same sound for e.

Short e and Long e

 **MY TURN** Read and write

| web | Steve | jet |

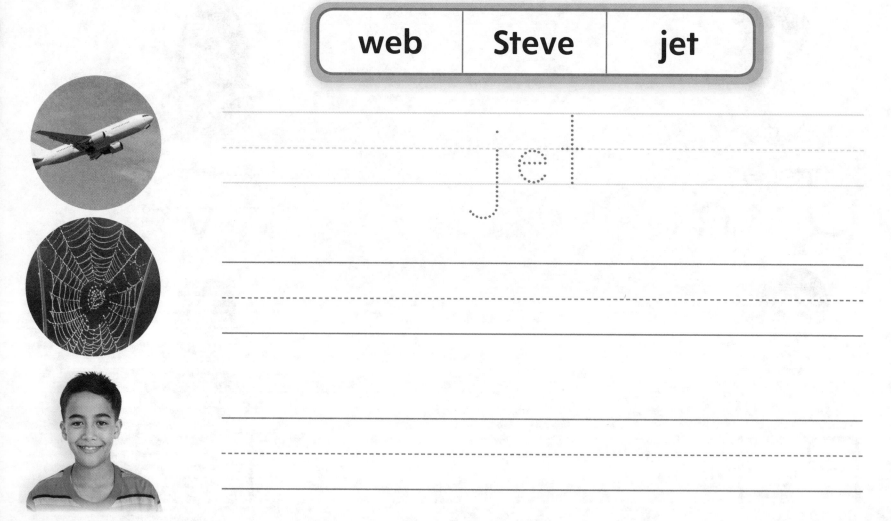

jet

Directions Remind students that the letter e can make the short e sound and the vowel pattern e_e can make the long e sound. Have students read the words in the word bank. Then have them write the word that names each picture on the lines.

Syllables

 Circle

Directions Have students identify, segment, and blend the syllables in each picture word. **Model:** Listen to this word: *kit-ten*, *kitten*. The word *kitten* has two syllables: *kit* and *ten*. Ask students to circle the picture words with two syllables.

Short e and Long e

 Read and circle

n e t

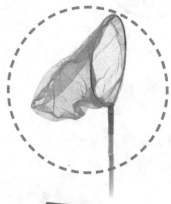

S t e v e

p e n

 96

Directions Remind students that the letter e can make the sound /e/ and the vowel pattern e_e can make the sound /ē/. Have students trace the letter or letters in each word and identify the vowel sound. Then ask them to read each word and circle the picture word that shows the word.

My Words to Know

black	brown	white

My Sentences to Read

I have the <u>white</u> flag.

I can take the black flag.

Where can the brown one go?

Directions Read the words aloud with students as they point to each word. Then have them read the sentences and underline the high-frequency words. Say: Now you will write one of the words on the lines. Tell students to form the letters correctly using appropriate directionality as they write the word.

Short e and Long e

 Read and write

98

Directions Have students name the pictures and trace the letter or letters in each word. Then have them read the words. Finally, have students write the words on the lines.

Jen and Pete

Highlight the words with the long **e** sound.

Jen and Pete had a brown drum.

Two hits said "Look!"

Four hits said "Come!"

AUDIO

Audio with Highlighting

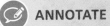
ANNOTATE

99

They wave a flag.

Black is for "Let us play!"

White is for "Help!"

Underline the words with the short **e** sound.

Now they send a text.

See!

Short e and Long e

 **Read**

 I am Pete.

 I am Eve.

 We have a pet.

 It is a hen.

Directions Remind students that the letter e can stand for the sound /e/ and the vowel pattern e_e can stand for the sound /ē/. Ask students to take turns reading the sentences with a partner.

Short e and Long e

 **MY TURN** (Circle) and <u>underline</u>

Can <u>Steve</u> (get) a pet?

Pete gave him a dog.

The dog is in the red pen.

They are at the vet.

Directions Have students read the sentences. Ask them to circle the words with short e and underline the words with long e.

My Learning Goal

I can read about the past.

Fiction

Fiction is a made-up story.

It has a setting, characters, and a plot.

Setting → It was <u>Saturday</u>.

Characters → <u>Dan</u> was at <u>home</u>.

Plot → He wanted to ask <u>Ben</u> to a party next week.

But his phone did not work.

So Dan sent Ben a letter.

 TURN and TALK How is the fiction story like narrative nonfiction?

Fiction Anchor Chart

Setting

Place

Time

Sunday	Monday	Tuesday	Wednesday	Thursday	Friday	Saturday
	1	2	3	4	5	(6)
7	8	9	10	11	12	13
14	15	16	17	18	19	20
21	22	23	24	25	26	27
28	29	30				

Grandma's Phone

Preview Vocabulary

farm

visit

pumpkin

Read

Read this story to find out what happens when a cell phone does not work.

Meet the Author

Ken Mochizuki was an actor before he began writing books for children. When he was a boy, he loved telling scary stories around a campfire.

106

Grandma's Phone

written by Ken Mochizuki

illustrated by Olga Skomorokhova

AUDIO

Audio with Highlighting

ANNOTATE

Grandma and Grandpa live on a farm.
Jess went to visit.

CLOSE READ

Where and when does the story happen? <u>Underline</u> the words that name the setting. Use the picture too.

Jess found a huge pumpkin.
"I want to tell Mom!" he said.

Jess tried to call Mom.
His phone didn't work.

CLOSE READ

Picture in your mind how Jess feels about his phone. Highlight the words that help you.

Jess tried to call Mom.
His phone still didn't work.

111

"Here," said Grandma.
"What is that?" Jess asked.

112

"It is a phone," said Grandma.
"Will it work?" Jess asked.

Jess tried to call Mom.
Grandma's phone worked!

114

CLOSE READ

Picture in your mind how Jess feels about Grandma's phone. Highlight the words that help you.

"Mom," said Jess.

He forgot about the pumpkin.

"You should see Grandma's cool phone!"

115

Read Together

Develop Vocabulary

farm	visit	pumpkin

 **MY TURN** Draw and write

_____

- -

_____

116

Directions Read the vocabulary words to students and discuss the meaning of each word. Then have students choose one vocabulary word to illustrate. Ask them to label their picture by writing the vocabulary word on the lines.

Check for Understanding

 Write

1. Could this story really happen? Why?

_____

- -

_____

2. How does the author describe the problem?

_____

- -

_____

3. How do the characters solve a problem?

_____

- -

_____

Directions Read the questions aloud and have students write their responses on the lines. Remind them to use text evidence.

Read Together

Describe Setting

The **setting** is when and where a story takes place.

 Write and circle

---

118

Directions Read aloud the information. Have students write where the story takes place in the first row and circle the picture that shows details about where the story takes place. Continue with the second row and when the story takes place. Remind students to look back at what they underlined in the text.

Visualize Details

 Draw

Directions Remind students that they can visualize, or create a picture in their mind, as they read. Ask: How does Jess feel when his cell phone does not work? How does he feel about Grandma's phone? Have students look at what they highlighted and discuss words the author uses that help them visualize the events. Ask them to think about the events and draw what they picture.

Reflect and Share

TURN and TALK How have phones changed?
How have cars changed? Talk to your partner.

Weekly Question

How has communication changed over time?

120

Directions Tell students they read about how phones have changed. Remind them they also read about how cars have changed. Say: You can respond to texts you have read by talking about what you learned. Have students provide an oral response to sources by discussing how phones and cars in the past are different from phones and cars today.

Read Together

I can use words to make connections.

My Learning Goal

Academic Vocabulary

time	change	discover	tradition

MY TURN Write

_____

Leaves _____ color in the fall.

Watching fireworks is my favorite _____.

Directions Read the sentences to students. Have them use context clues to determine which word best completes each sentence. Ask students to respond by writing the words on the lines.

Spell Words

 Sort and spell

met	red	black
pen	brown	net

met

122

Directions Say: Short e is often spelled e in words with three letters. Some words do not follow a pattern, so we have to remember how to spell them. Have students determine if each word follows the CVC pattern. Then have them spell and write the CVC words in the left column and the high-frequency words in the right column.

Read Together

Read Like a Writer, Write for a Reader

MY TURN Write

1. What words help you know that this is a third-person text?

_____

- -

_____

2. What else might Jess do at the farm? Use words such as **Jess** and **he** to tell about the event.

_____

- -

_____

Directions Remind students that a narrator tells a story. Say: Sometimes the narrator is not a character in the story. The narrator uses characters' names and words such as *his* or *her* to tell about events. Have students listen to and experience third-person text as you read a page from the story. Then read the items and have students write their responses.

123

End Punctuation

Telling sentences end with a period.

Asking sentences end with a question mark.

Exclamations end with an exclamation point.

Adam wants a pumpkin.

Which one is best?

It is heavy!

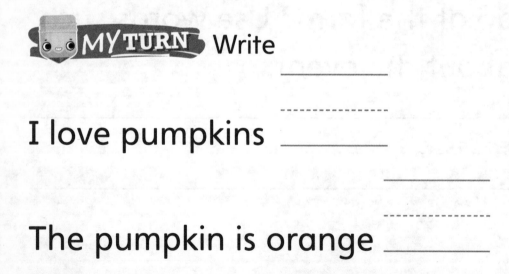 MY TURN Write _____

I love pumpkins _____

_____

The pumpkin is orange _____

Directions Read the information to students. Then read the exclamatory and declarative sentences at the bottom of the page. Have students edit the sentences by writing the correct punctuation mark at the end of each one.

I can write a story about myself.

What Happens First

The beginning of a personal narrative tells what happens first.

It often tells about a problem.

 Draw

Directions Say: Authors organize the ideas in a personal narrative. They tell about events in the order they happened. Have students think about what happens first in their personal narrative. Have them organize their ideas by drawing what happens first.

What Happens Next

The middle of a personal narrative tells what happens next.

 Draw

Directions Remind students that authors organize their ideas by telling about events in the order they happened. Have students think about what happens next in their personal narrative. Have them organize their ideas by drawing what happens next.

What Happens Last

The ending of a personal narrative tells what happens last.
It often tells the resolution.

 Draw

Directions Remind students that a resolution is how a problem is solved, or fixed. Have students think about what happens last in their personal narrative, including how they solved a problem. Have them organize their ideas by drawing what happens last. Direct students to compose beginning, middle, and ending events for their personal narrative.

Then and Now

Life was different for children in the past.

Long ago many children learned in schools with only one room.

What was life like in the past?

Many children played with handmade toys.

 Write

_____

- -

_____

Directions Read the text and have students look at the pictures. Ask them to discuss how life in the past was similar to and different from life today. Then have students interact with the source by writing about one way their life would be different if they had lived in the past.

129

Words for Pp, Yy

 Read and write

That is my _en.

pen

I like the _ak.

Pat said _es.

Pam got the _in.

Directions Remind students that *p* stands for /p/ and *y* stands for /y/. Ask students to read each sentence and name the picture to complete the sentence. Then have them write the word for the picture on the lines.

Words for Short and Long i

 **Read and write**

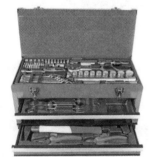

I like the  .

Kim had a _____ .

I will ride the _____ .

Directions Remind students that the vowel pattern *i_e* makes the long *i* vowel sound and the CVC pattern makes the short *i* vowel sound. Then have students read each sentence and write the word for the picture to complete the sentence. Have partners take turns reading the completed sentences.

Words for Short and Long i, Pp, Yy

 Read

 Zip on a line.

 Step in time.

 Nod yes.

 Smile at a pup.

132

Directions Remind students that the vowel pattern *i_e* makes the long *i* vowel sound and the CVC pattern makes the short *i* vowel sound. Also review that *p* stands for /p/ and *y* stands for /y/. Have partners take turns reading the sentences.

My Words to Know

good	open	could

My Sentences to Read

 MY TURN

We o̲p̲e̲n̲ the box.

Could we play with it?

Yes! It is still good.

Directions Say: We have to remember and practice some words, such as *open*. Have students read the high-frequency words. Then have them read the sentences and underline the high-frequency words in the sentences.

Sentences I Can Read

 Read and write

☐ Tim had a big dime.
☒ Tim had a big bike.

☐ I will play with the kite.
☐ I will play with the vine.

☐ We can ride up the hill.
☐ We can hike up the hill.

Directions Ask students to look at the first picture. Then have them read the first set of sentences. Ask students to write an X in the box for the sentence that tells about the picture. Continue with the other pictures and sentences.

The Past and Now

Highlight the words that end with the **p** sound.

Open up the past.

What do you see?

They could tap and run.

Can we? Yes, we can!

 AUDIO

Audio with Highlighting

 ANNOTATE

They made a <u>kite</u>.

They ride a <u>bike</u>.

Underline the words with the long **i** sound.

They had a good time.

Do we? Yes, we do!

137

Sentences I Can Read

 Read and write

run	time	pig

Get the ꓸꓸꓸpig , Rob.

They _____ a lot.

It is _____ for a nap!

Directions Ask students to read the words and sentences. Then have them write the words to complete the sentences. Finally, have students read the completed sentences.

Sentences I Can Read

 **MY TURN** Read and write

can	ride.	They

Rob and the pig wake up.

They see Pat on Mike.

How will they get home?

Directions Ask students to read the sentences. Have them use the words in the box to write the last sentence for the story. Alternatively, students may wish to write their own last sentence.

Read
Together

My Learning Goal

I can read narrative nonfiction.

SPOTLIGHT ON GENRE

Narrative Nonfiction

A **biography** is a kind of narrative nonfiction.

It tells about important events in the life of a person.

It may have a **time line** to show when the events happened.

July 16, 1969   July 20, 1969

TURN and TALK Talk about the events on the time line.

Directions Read the genre information to students. Say: Narrative nonfiction can use titles and graphics, such as time lines and pictures, to give information about the people, places, and events. Have partners discuss the events shown on the time line.

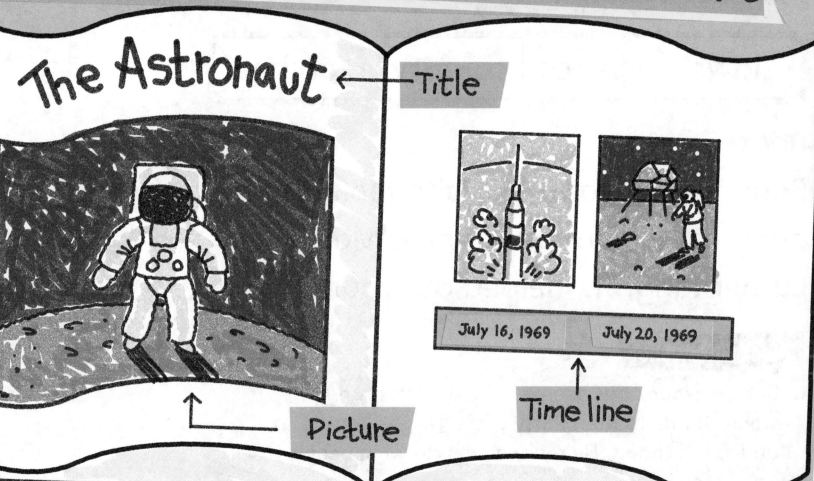

Narrative Nonfiction Anchor Chart

The Astronaut ← Title

Picture

July 16, 1969   July 20, 1969

Time line

Changing Laws, Changing Lives: Martin Luther King, Jr.

Preview Vocabulary

laws	speech	country	marched

Read

Read the title and text and look at the pictures to learn about how Martin Luther King, Jr., helped our country.

Meet the Author

Eric Velasquez has been writing and illustrating stories for more than thirty years. He also teaches art and visits schools. He really enjoys drawing people in his sketchbook.

Changing Laws, Changing Lives: Martin Luther King, Jr.

written by Eric Velasquez

AUDIO
Audio with Highlighting

ANNOTATE

Martin Luther King, Jr., was born in 1929.
He lived in Atlanta, Georgia.
Martin grew up to be an important man.

During his life, he saw African Americans being treated unfairly. He wanted to help them.

African Americans could not drink from some fountains.
They could not eat at some tables.

CLOSE READ

How were African Americans treated at restaurants long ago? Highlight the words.

They could not sit at the front of a bus. They could not even play with some of their friends!

147

Martin was sad.
He would change things.
He marched. He made speeches.

CLOSE READ

How are people treated at restaurants today? Highlight the words. Use the picture too.

Now people drink from any fountain.
People eat at any table.

People sit anywhere on a bus.
People can be friends with anyone.
Martin made our country better.

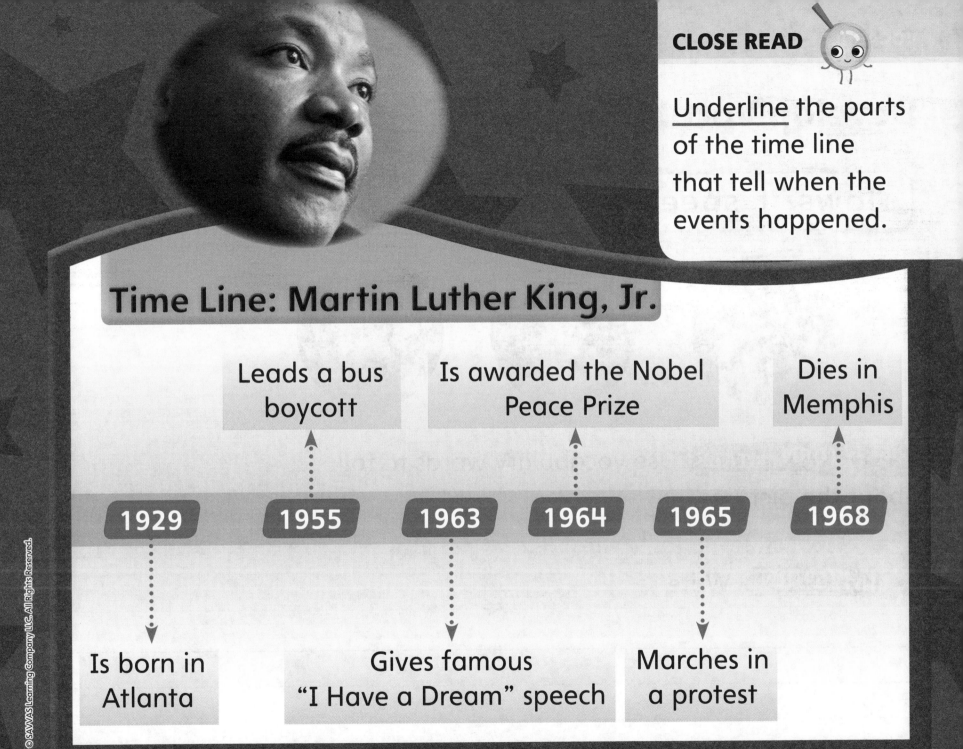

CLOSE READ

Underline the parts of the time line that tell when the events happened.

Time Line: Martin Luther King, Jr.

Leads a bus boycott

Is awarded the Nobel Peace Prize

Dies in Memphis

1929 **1955** **1963** **1964** **1965** **1968**

Is born in Atlanta

Gives famous "I Have a Dream" speech

Marches in a protest

Develop Vocabulary

| laws | speech | country | marched |

 **Use vocabulary words to talk about the pictures.**

 MY TURN Write

_____

- -

_____

152

Directions Read aloud the vocabulary words and have students use the words to talk to a partner about the pictures. Then have students dictate or write a sentence using at least one vocabulary word.

Check for Understanding

 **MY TURN** Write

1. How do you know this is a biography?

_____

_____

2. How does the author describe Martin?

_____

_____

3. Why did Martin want to change things?

_____

_____

Directions Read each question aloud and have students write their responses. Remind them to use evidence from the text.

Find Text Features

Text features help readers learn information.

One kind of text feature is a time line.

A **time line** shows when events happen.

 Draw and write

_____

- -

_____

154

Directions Read aloud the information about time lines. Then have students look back at what they underlined in the text. Ask them to draw an event from the time line and write when the event happened on the lines. Discuss the author's purpose and how the time line helps the author achieve that purpose.

Create New Understandings

 Draw

Directions Tell students that they can combine details they read in a text to learn something new. Have them synthesize information from the text to understand how life has changed. Ask students to draw pictures that show what life was like in the past and how it has changed. Remind them to look back at what they highlighted.

Reflect and Share

 MY TURN Write

_____

1. _____

_____

_____

_____

2. _____

Weekly Question

What was life like in the past?

Directions Tell students they read about a real person, Martin Luther King, Jr. Ask them to think of another real person they have read about. Say: You can respond to texts by writing about what you have learned. Have students respond to sources by writing one detail they learned about Martin Luther King, Jr., and one detail about another real person.

Read Together

I can use words to tell about narrative nonfiction.

My Learning Goal

Academic Vocabulary

time	change	discover	tradition

 Circle

I _____ my clothes before school.

changer	changed

The coach used a _____ during the race.

timer	timed

Directions Say: Adding a word part changes the meaning of a word. The ending *-ed* changes a verb to tell about an action that already happened. The ending *-er* means "something that." It changes a verb into a noun. Read the sentences to students. Have them circle the correct form of the word to complete each sentence.

157

Spell Words

 Sort and spell

in	good	it
if	is	it open

in

_____

_____

_____

_____

Directions Say: Short *i* is often spelled *i* in words with two letters. Some words do not follow a pattern, so we have to remember how to spell them. Have students determine if each word follows the VC pattern. Then have them spell and write the VC words in the left column and the high-frequency words in the right column.

Read Like a Writer, Write for a Reader

 **MY TURN** Write

1. Find words in the text that tell why the author thinks Martin was an important person.

_____

- -

_____

2. Why do you think Martin was an important person?

_____

- -

_____

_____

- -

_____

Directions Say: Sometimes authors tell what they think about someone or something. They give reasons to support their ideas. Read the first item to students and have them look back at the text to find an answer. Then read the second item and have students write their response. Remind them to use text evidence.

Question Words

A question begins with a question word.

It ends with a question mark.

Some question words are **who, what, where, when, why,** and **how.**

Who is in the picture**?**

 **TURN and TALK** Ask questions using question words.

 **MY TURN** Write

Who	When	How

_____   _____

- -

_____ was Martin born_____

Directions Read aloud the information and discuss the question words with students. Have partners take turns asking questions using the question words. Then ask students to edit the sentence at the bottom of the page by writing a question word at the beginning and adding a punctuation mark at the end.

I can write a story about myself.

My Learning Goal

Edit for Punctuation Marks

A complete sentence ends with a **punctuation mark.**

Telling sentences end with a **period.**

MY TURN Cross out and write

_____

- - - - - - - - - - - - -

Tim and Pam go to camp? _____

_____

- - - - - - - - - - -

Nev plays the flute. _____

_____

- - - - - - - - - -

Pablo likes to skate! _____

Directions Read aloud the sentences and have students determine if they end with the correct punctuation marks. Ask them to edit the sentences by crossing out the punctuation marks that are not correct and writing the correct punctuation marks on the lines. Have students edit their personal narratives for punctuation marks at the end of declarative sentences.

161

Edit for Verbs

A **verb** is an action word.

Verbs that tell about an action in the past often end with **ed.**

 **MY TURN** (Circle) and write

Dad and I walk a lot.

_____

- -

_____

We look at the monkeys.

_____

- -

_____

162

Directions Say: Personal narratives often use verbs that tell about actions in the past. Have students edit the draft by circling the present-tense verb in each sentence and rewriting it as a past-tense verb. Direct students to edit the verbs in their personal narratives.

Edit for Subjective and Possessive Pronouns

A **pronoun** takes the place of a noun in a sentence.

Some pronouns tell who a sentence is about.

Some pronouns tell that something belongs to someone.

 **MY TURN** Match

John likes to paint.   his

This is John's brush.   He

Directions Review subjective and possessive pronouns with students. Then have them edit the sentences by drawing a line from each sentence to the pronoun that could replace the underlined noun. Ask students to edit their personal narratives for subjective and possessive pronouns.

A Family Tradition

My family goes camping
each Fourth of July.
Our tradition keeps going
though years have gone by.

We hike, and we sing
by the campfire's glow,
then wrap up the night
with a fireworks show!

What can we learn from family traditions?

 **Draw**

Directions Read the poem aloud and have students look at the pictures. Ask them to talk about how their own family traditions are similar to and different from the tradition described in the poem. Then have students draw a picture to show a family tradition.

165

Words for Dd, Ff, Vv

 **MY TURN** Read and write

It can _ig.

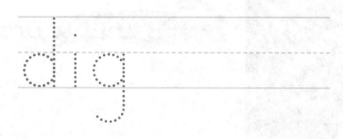
dig

We have _un.

The _et is with a cat.

Directions Ask students to name each picture. Then have them read each sentence and say the picture word to complete the sentence. Finally, have them write the word for the picture on the lines.

Words for Short e

 **MY TURN** Read and (circle)

I (get) in the bed .

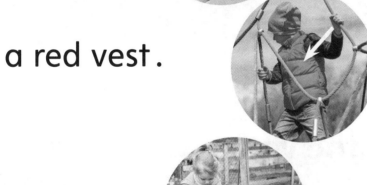

He had a red vest .

She fed the hen .

Sam went on a sled .

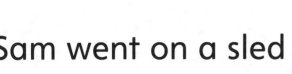

167

Directions Point out the word *get* in the first sentence and remind students that the letter *e* can make the sound /e/. Have students read the sentences and circle the words with the short *e* sound.

Words for Short e, Dd, Ff, Vv

 Read

 Where did Dad go?

 Dad went in the fast van.

 He and Fin are at the vet.

 Fin is a fun dog!

168

Directions Remind students that e can make the sound /e/, d stands for /d/, f stands for /f/, and v stands for /v/. Then have partners take turns reading the sentences.

My Words to Know

| want | every | please |

My Sentences to Read

I <u>want</u> to help every time.

Please let me help!

Directions Say: There are some words we have to remember and practice. Listen as I read these words: *want, every, please.* Have students read the high-frequency words. Then have them read the sentences and underline the high-frequency words in the sentences.

Sentences I Can Read

 Read and match

Ted had a big fan.

Dot can dig.

We go in the van.

Dan fed the pet.

170

Directions Have students read the sentences. Then have them draw a line from each sentence to the matching picture.

We Have Fun

Highlight the words with the short **e** sound.

Every June we go west on a jet.

We have a fun trip.

 AUDIO
Audio with Highlighting

 ANNOTATE

We fix up a home.

We want to help.

We go to the lake in a van.

We get to d<u>i</u>v<u>e</u> and swim.

Underline the words with the **d** sound.

We have a big ham.

Please sit and dine with us.

173

Sentences I Can Read

 MY TURN Read and write

| dime | van | pen | fun |

Ted is in a red _van_.

It is _____ to swim.

She had one _____.

The pig went in the _____.

Directions Ask students to read the words and sentences. Then have them write the word that best completes each sentence on the lines. Finally, have students read the completed sentences.

Sentences I Can Read

 Read and write

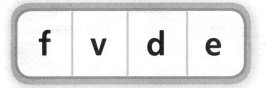

I hit it over the net.

Dad can ___ig a hole.

It is hot and we want a ___an.

Please let us ride in the ___an.

Directions Have students identify the letters in the letter bank. Then have them read the sentences. Explain that students will use the letters to complete words in the sentences. Remind them to make sure the sentences make sense when they complete the words.

My Learning Goal   I can read about the past.

Fiction

Fiction stories tell about made-up characters.

They often have a **theme**, or a big idea.

Made-up Characters — The Johnson family was having a special dinner. Grandma brought chicken. Uncle Jeff brought mashed potatoes. Everyone ate and talked.

Theme — The Johnsons like spending time together.

TURN and TALK How is this story like a narrative nonfiction story? How is it different?

176

Directions Read aloud the genre information and model text. Have students discuss the topic of the story and determine the basic theme. Then have them talk about how fiction is similar to and different from narrative nonfiction.

Read Together

Fiction Anchor Chart

Theme

Characters

Tempura, Tempera

Preview Vocabulary

| served | sailed | shared | brought |

Read

What questions do you have before you read the story?

Meet the Illustrator

Teresa Martinez illustrates books for children. She grew up in Mexico, where she liked to play in the river and walk with the cows.

Directions Have students listen to the title and look at the illustration on the title page. Ask them to generate questions about the text before reading.

Genre Fiction

Tempura, Tempera

written by Lyn Miller-Lachmann   illustrated by Teresa Martinez

AUDIO

Audio with Highlighting

ANNOTATE

It was Grandfather's birthday.
He is from Portugal.

Haruko came to dinner.
She is from Japan.

Haruko brought eight pretty flowers.
"Eight is lucky in Japan," she said.

VOCABULARY IN CONTEXT

Which words help you understand what **delicious** means? Highlight the words.

Teresa said, "Mother made fried fish. It is delicious. Grandfather loves it."

Mother served the fish.
She served beans.

CLOSE READ

What questions could you ask about these pages? Highlight the parts of the text you have questions about.

"This looks like tempura!" said Haruko. Grandfather said, "Tempura comes from my home. We call it *tempera*."

"A long time ago, sailors left
Portugal," explained Teresa.
"They sailed to Japan.
They shared their tempera."

CLOSE READ

What is this story about? <u>Underline</u> clues from the text that help you answer the question.

"The Japanese liked tempera then," said Teresa.

"And I like tempura now!" said Haruko.

Develop Vocabulary

 **MY TURN** Write

| served | sailed | shared | brought |

Haruko _____ flowers for Grandfather.

Mother _____ tempura for dinner.

 188

Directions Read aloud the vocabulary words. Then read the sentences aloud. Have students complete each sentence by writing the vocabulary word that best completes it on the lines.

Read
Together

Check for Understanding

 Write

1. What happens after Mother serves dinner?

_____

- -

_____

2. How does the author describe the food?

_____

- -

_____

3. How do the characters share traditions?

_____

- -

_____

Directions Read aloud the questions and have students write their responses. Remind them to use text evidence.

Determine Theme

The **theme** is the big idea of a text.

 Draw

190

Directions Read the information aloud to students. Say: You can talk about the topic, or what the story is all about, and use what you know from your own life to help you understand the theme. Have students discuss topics and determine the basic theme of the story. Remind them to look back at what they underlined in the text. Then have students draw a picture to show the theme.

Ask and Answer Questions

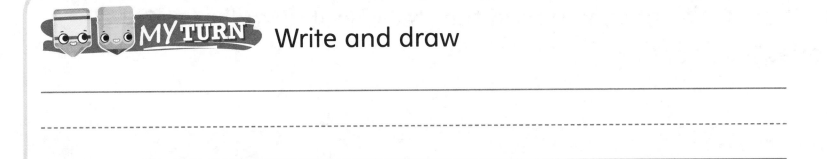 **MY TURN** Write and draw

_____

- -

_____

Directions Remind students that they can ask and answer questions about what they read to help them deepen understanding and gain information. Have students dictate or write a question they had about the story during reading or generate a new question about the text. Prompt them to look back at what they highlighted. Then have students draw a picture to answer their question.

Reflect and Share

TURN and TALK What tradition does the story tell about? What other stories have you read that tell about a tradition? Retell the stories to a partner.

First

Next

Last

Weekly Question

What can we learn from family traditions?

192

Directions Tell students they read about characters who eat a special kind of food. Ask them to think of another story they have read that tells about a tradition. Have students retell the events in the stories. Say: When you retell a story, you tell the important events. Then have partners respond to sources by discussing the traditions in each story.

Read Together

I can use words to make connections.

My Learning Goal

Academic Vocabulary

| time | change | discover | tradition |

TURN and TALK Talk about the pictures.

Directions Have students talk about the pictures with a partner. Remind them to use the Academic Vocabulary words.

Spell Words

 **Sort and spell**

bed	fed	vet
want	please	den

b e d

194

Directions Say: Short e is often spelled e in words with three letters. Some words do not follow a pattern, so we have to remember how to spell them. Have students determine if each word follows the CVC pattern. Then have them spell and write the CVC words in the left column and the high-frequency words in the right column.

Read Like a Writer, Write for a Reader

 Write

1. How does the author use pictures to help you understand the end of the story?

_____

- -

_____

_____

- -

_____

2. What picture could you add to help readers better understand the story?

_____

- -

_____

Directions Have students discuss how the author uses graphic features, such as maps and illustrations, to achieve a specific purpose and help readers understand the text. Read aloud the questions and have students write their responses.

Question Words

Questions begin with a **question word**.
They end with a question mark.

Where are they?

What do they eat?

 **MY TURN** (Circle) and write

_____ is the library _____

Who	**Where**

_____ book should I get _____

What	**When**

196

Directions Read aloud the information and review the question words *who, what, where, when, why,* and *how* with students. Then read the sentence stems. Have students edit the sentences by circling the correct question word for the beginning and writing a punctuation mark at the end of each sentence.

I can write a story about myself.

My Learning Goal

Edit for Capitalization

The first letter in a name is always **capitalized.**

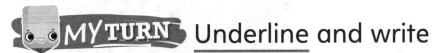 Underline and write

I saw <u>mike</u> at the zoo.

_____

He was with his sister abby. _____

_____

His dog max was there too. _____

Directions Have students edit the draft by underlining the name in each sentence and rewriting it with correct capitalization on the lines. Direct students to edit for capitalization in their personal narratives.

Read Together

Edit for Spelling

Good writers check that they have spelled words correctly.

 Circle and write

The lion is in the deen.

_____

- -

_____

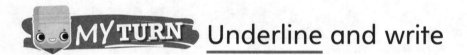 Underline and write

Can we pleas see the monkey now?

_____

- -

_____

198

Directions Tell students they have learned spelling patterns that can help them check their spelling. Say: You have learned that short e is often spelled e in words with three letters. Have students circle the misspelled word in the first sentence and write the correct spelling on the lines. Then tell students they have also learned to spell some words that do not follow a pattern, such as *please* and *now*. Have students underline the misspelled word in the second sentence and write the correct spelling on the lines.

Assessment

Here is what you have learned to do in this unit!

- ☐ Write about real people

- ☐ Write about real settings

- ☐ Write about real events

- ☐ Edit for nouns and pronouns

- ☐ Capitalize names

Directions Read the list with students and discuss the items. Encourage students to ask questions if they do not understand the information. You may wish to review other skills students have learned in this unit, such as generating and organizing ideas and editing for verbs and end punctuation marks.

UNIT THEME
Then and Now

 **TURN and TALK**

Go back to each text and tell one thing you learned about the past. Use the Weekly Questions to help you.

BOOK CLUB

WEEK 3

Grandma's Phone

How has communication changed over time?

WEEK 2

Uncovering the Past

How do we learn about the past?

BOOK CLUB

WEEK 1

Cars Are Always Changing

Why is it important to make inventions better?

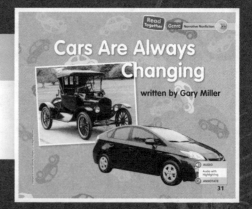

200

WEEK 4

Changing Laws, Changing Lives: Martin Luther King, Jr.

What was life like in the past?

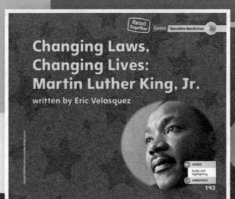

Changing Laws, Changing Lives: Martin Luther King, Jr.
written by Eric Velasquez

Read Together

WEEK 6

BOOK CLUB

WEEK 5

BOOK CLUB

Tempura, Tempera

What can we learn from family traditions?

Tempura, Tempera
written by Lyn Miller-Lachmann   illustrated by Teresa Martinez

Essential Question

What can we learn from the past?

Project

WEEK 6

Now it is time to apply what you have learned about the past in your **WEEK 6 PROJECT: Looking Back.**

201

Words for Hh, Xx

 Read and write

She had a _at.

hat

The dog is in a bo_.

The fo_ can

have the _am.

202

Directions Have students read each sentence and name the picture to complete the sentence. Then ask them to write the words for the pictures on the lines.

Words for Short and Long u

 Read and circle

Jan is ____ in her blue dress.   cut   cute

I can play the ____.   flute   fun

The dog is in the ____.   tub   tube

Directions Remind students that the letter *u* can make the short vowel sound /u/ and the vowel pattern *u_e* can make the long vowel sound /ū/. Have students read each sentence and the answer choices. Ask them to circle the word that best completes the sentence.

Spell Words

 Sort and spell

sun	bug	this
may	tug	nut

sun

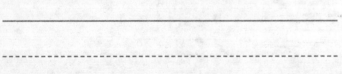

204

Directions Say: Short *u* is often spelled *u* in words with three letters. Some words do not follow a pattern, so we have to remember how to spell them. Have students determine if each word follows the CVC pattern. Then have them spell and write the CVC words in the left column and the high-frequency words in the right column.

My Words to Know

may	this	round

My Sentences to Read

 Underline

They made a <u>round</u> ham.

May I have some of this?

Directions Remind students that we need to remember and practice some words. Have students read the high-frequency words. Then have them read the sentences and underline the high-frequency words in the sentences.

Words for Short and Long u, Hh, Xx

MY TURN Read and match

a fox in a box

a cute hat

a red hen

a little cub

a yellow sun

Directions Have students tell what they see in the pictures. Then ask them to read the phrases and draw a line from each phrase to the matching picture.

A Home in the Past

June is up with the sun.

She will help Bess.

 AUDIO
Audio with Highlighting
ANNOTATE

207

June will hum a tune with Mom.

They get sod for the fire.

They set this log in the box.

Now June and Max may run.

Underline the words
with the **h** sound.

Mom made a round ham.

Pop is home!

Now they can have it.

Sentences I Can Read

 MY TURN Read and write

☒ Can you fix the flat tire?
☐ Can you mix the flat tire?

☐ He had a huge cap.
☐ He had a huge cup.

☐ They like the cute ham.
☐ They like the cute home.

210

Directions Have students tell what they see in each picture. Then ask them to read each pair of sentences and write an X in the box by the sentence that tells about the picture.

Sentences I Can Read

 Read and (circle)

The bug is cute.

He can fix this.

We like ham.

Directions Ask students to read the first sentence. Then have them look at the pictures and circle the one that matches the sentence. Continue with the remaining sentences and pictures.

Looking Back

Look at the picture. How did children live in the past?

TURN and TALK Talk about how children from the past and children today are alike and different.

Directions Have students talk with a partner about the children in the picture. Ask them to tell how children in the past and children today are similar and different.

Use Words

COLLABORATE Talk to your partner. What questions do you have about life in the past? Use new academic words.

My Research Plan Fill in the steps. Check each box as you do your project.

☐ Choose a person to interview.

☐ _____

_____

☐ _____

Directions Have partners discuss what they want to learn about life in the past. Encourage them to use Academic Vocabulary as they generate questions. Then help students develop, and then follow, a research plan for their project. **Say:** Think about the steps you need to follow for your project and write them on the lines. Then check the boxes as you do the steps.

213

What Is It About?

Informational texts have a title and main idea.

The **title** often names the topic of the text.

The **main idea** is what the text is mostly about.

My Dad

My dad was outside a lot when he was a kid. He played baseball with his friends. He found rocks for his rock collection.

214

Directions Read aloud the information and the model text. Ask students to find and circle the title of the text. Have them talk about what they learn about the text from the title. Then have students find and underline the main idea of the text.

Conduct an Interview

RESEARCH

You can gather information about life in the past by talking to older people. You can interview them by asking questions and explaining what you wish to learn.

 **MY TURN** Write

_____

_____

 **COLLABORATE** Talk about questions you can ask.

Directions Say: In an interview, you ask someone questions to learn information. Explain that students will interview an older family member about what life was like when he or she was a child. Ask students to write the name of the family member they will interview. Then have partners think about what they want to know and generate questions for their interview.

Take Notes

What did you do for fun?

played jacks and
other games

  Write or draw

Directions Read aloud the research example at the top of the page. Then have students follow the example to take their own notes as they interview an older family member about what life was like when he or she was a child.

Revise and Edit

Add details to make your writing better.

You can **add details** in pictures.

You can **add details** in words.

| She played games. |

| She played jacks. |

 **Write**

Directions Read aloud the revision example and discuss why *jacks* is a better detail than *games*. Have students look back at their writing. Ask them to follow the example to revise a sentence by adding details in words.

Share

Follow the rules for speaking and listening.

Use complete sentences.

Listen actively.

Reflect

 Circle

Did I learn about the past?	
Did I use complete sentences?	

Directions Have students review the listening and speaking behaviors before sharing their project. After they present, have students reflect on their project.

Reflect on Your Reading

 Write

I learned

Reflect on Your Writing

 Write

I liked writing about

Directions Have students reflect on their reading and writing in this unit.

How to Use a Picture Dictionary

This is a picture of the word.

This is the word you are learning.

first

 Draw

Directions Remind students that they can use a picture dictionary to find words. Say: The topic of this picture dictionary is sequence. Listen as I read the words. Use the pictures to help you understand the meanings of the words. Have students identify the word *before* and use it in a sentence. Then have them draw a picture that shows the meaning of the word.

Sequence

next

then

last

before

after

How to Use Digital Resources

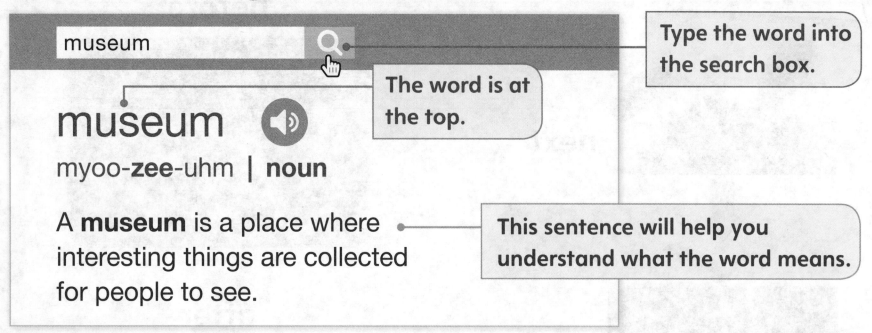

museum

museum

myoo-**zee**-uhm | **noun**

A **museum** is a place where interesting things are collected for people to see.

Type the word into the search box.

The word is at the top.

This sentence will help you understand what the word means.

 **MY TURN** Draw

Directions Tell students they can use an online dictionary or resource to find words that are not in the glossary. Say: First, type the word you are looking for in the search box. Then hit return. Have students find the word *fountain* using an online dictionary and draw a picture that shows the meaning of the word.

Bb

brought If you **brought** something, you took it with you.

brushes **Brushes** are tools used for cleaning.

Cc

CD player A **CD player** is a device that plays sound from a plastic disc.

change When things **change**, they become different.

country A **country** is an area where people live that has a government.

crank A **crank** is a handle you turn to start a machine.

Dd

discover When you **discover** something, you find or see it for the first time.

Ee

engine An **engine** is a machine that makes something work.

Ff

farm A **farm** is a place where people grow crops or raise animals.

Ll

laws **Laws** are rules made by a country.

Mm

marched If someone **marched,** he or she participated in an organized walk with a group of people to support something.

Pp

past The **past** is all the time that has gone by.

pumpkin A **pumpkin** is a round, orange fruit that grows on a vine.

225

Rr

radio A **radio** is a device that plays sound carried by signals.

Ss

sailed Someone who **sailed** traveled on a boat.

scientists **Scientists** are people who study the natural world.

served If you **served**, you set food out for people to eat.

shared If you **shared**, you let others use or have something.

shovels **Shovels** are tools used to dig.

speech A **speech** is a formal talk to a group of people.

Tt

time **Time** is what we measure in seconds, minutes, hours, days, months, and years.

tradition A **tradition** is a belief or custom handed down from one person to another.

Vv

visit When you **visit**, you go to see someone or something.

Photographs

Photo locators denoted as follows Top (T), Center (C), Bottom (B), Left (L), Right (R), Background (Bkgd)

5 DutchScenery/Getty Images, Vintage Images/Alamy Stock Photo, Prudencio Alvarez/123RF; 6 Picksell/Shutterstock, Reg Lancaster/ Getty Images; 8 (BL) Konstantin Tronin/Shutterstock, (Bkgd) Rawpixel/Shutterstock; 9 (TL) DutchScenery/Getty Images, Vintage Images/Alamy Stock Photo, Prudencio Alvarez/123RF, (CL) Picksell/ Shutterstock, Reg Lancaster/Getty Images; 10 (R) Hero Images Inc./ Alamy Stock Photo, (L) Blaj Gabriel/Shutterstock; 12 (L) Joyfuldesigns/Shutterstock, (R) MBI/Alamy Stock Photo; 13 (BCR) Microgen/Shutterstock, (BR) Stockbroker/123RF, (CL) Gelpi/ Shutterstock, (CR) Gelpi/Shutterstock, (TR) Monticello/Shutterstock; 14 Anneka/Shutterstock; 15 (Bkgd) Toria/Shutterstock, (CR) Yougoigo/Shutterstock; 16 (BCL) Philipimage/Shutterstock, (BCR) Dcwcreations/Shutterstock, (BL) Shtanzman/123RF, (BR) Andrey Kuzmin/Shutterstock, (TCL) Dny3d/Shutterstock, (TCR) Eric Isselee/ Shutterstock, (TL) Josefauer/Shutterstock, (TR) Bragin Alexey/ Shutterstock; 17 (TR) Boleslaw Kubica/Shutterstock, (BL) Topseller/ Shutterstock, (BR) Dny3d/Shutterstock, (BC) Paulo Resende/ Shutterstock; 18 (B) Paulo Resende/Shutterstock, (T) Philipimage/ Shutterstock; 19 (BCL) Hong Vo/Shutterstock, (BCR) Pernsanitfoto/ Shutterstock, (BL) Dny3d/Shutterstock, (BR) Paul Orr/Shutterstock, (TCL) Africa Studio/Shutterstock, (TCR) Deep OV/Shutterstock, (TL) Insago/Shutterstock, (TR) Africa Studio/Shutterstock; 20 (BC) Rawpixel/Shutterstock, (BL) Lisa A. Svara/Shutterstock, (BR) Insago/ Shutterstock, (TC) Boleslaw Kubica/Shutterstock, (TL) Pernsanitfoto/ Shutterstock, (TR) Africa Studio/Shutterstock; 22 (BL) Carsten Reisinger/Shutterstock, (BR) Ever/Shutterstock, (CL) Insago/ Shutterstock, (CR) Ronnachai Palas/Shutterstock, (TL) My Good Images/Shutterstock, (TR) Josefauer/Shutterstock; 27 (TCR) Elena Dijour/Shutterstock, (TCL) Catalin Petolea/Shutterstock, (TL) Eric Isselee/Shutterstock; 30 (TCL) Kvsan/Shutterstock, (TCR) DutchScenery/Getty Images, (TL) Vintage Images/Alamy Stock Photo, (TR) Prudencio Alvarez/123RF; 31 (L) Performance Image/ Alamy Stock Photo, (R) Michael Doolittle/Alamy Stock Photo, (Bkgd) Cozy nook/Shutterstock; 32 LUke1138/Getty Images; 33 (L) Vintage Images/Alamy Stock Photo, (BR) Neirfy/123RF; 34 Mary Evans Picture Library/Alamy Stock Photo; 35 (C) Wicki58/Getty Images, (T) Chronicle/Alamy Stock Photo; 36 Everett Collection Inc/

Alamy Stock Photo; 37 (T) DutchScenery/Getty Images, (B) Trait2lumiere/Getty Images; 38 (T) Prudencio Alvarez/123RF, (B) Heritage Images/Getty Images; 39 Victor Habbick Visions/Getty Images; 40 (BL) Prudencio Alvarez/123RF, (BR) DutchScenery/Getty Images, (TL) Kvsan/Shutterstock, (TR) Vintage Images/Alamy Stock Photo; 48 (B) Dotshock/Shutterstock, (T) Andrey Armyagov/ Shutterstock; 51 (C) Praweena style/Shutterstock, (L) XiXinXing/ Shutterstock, (R) Boris Diakovsky/Shutterstock; 53 (L) Tom Wang/ Shutterstock, (R) Microgen/Shutterstock; 54 (BL) Robynrg/ Shutterstock, (TCR) Patrick Bombaert/Shutterstock, (BR) Olga Kovalenko/Shutterstock, (BCL) Triff/Shutterstock, (BCR) Stockagogo, Craig Barhorst/Shutterstock, (TCL) Alex Tarassov/Shutterstock, (TL) Africa Studio/Shutterstock, (TR) Nick Biebach/123RF; 55 (BCR) Jelena Aloskina/Shutterstock, (BCR) Sergio Schnitzler/Shutterstock, (B) Robynrg/Shutterstock, (TCR) Patrick Bombaert/Shutterstock, (TCL) 123RF, (T) Triff/Shutterstock; 56 (B) Warawanai Neko/ Shutterstock, (C) Robynrg/Shutterstock, (T) Timmary/123RF; 58 (BC) Olga Kovalenko/Shutterstock, (BL) Paulo Resende/Shutterstock, (BR) Patrick Bombaert/Shutterstock, (TC) Phant/Shutterstock, (TL) DenisNata/Shutterstock, (TR) Robyn Mackenzie/123RF; 65 (B) Antonio Gravante/Shutterstock, (C) Prasert Wongchindawest/ Shutterstock, (T) Monkey Business Images/Shutterstock; 66 Dennis Hallinan/Alamy Stock Photo; 68 (TC) Masarik/Shutterstock, (TL) Openfinal/Shutterstock, (TR) Masarik/Shutterstock; 78 (TR) Openfinal/Shutterstock, (CR, BR) Masarik/Shutterstock; 83 (T) Microgen/Shutterstock, (B) Carlos E. Santa Maria/Shutterstock; 87 (C) Jack Schiffer/Shutterstock, (L) Sergey Nivens/Shutterstock, (R) Takacs Szabolcs/Shutterstock; 88 (L) Anyka/123RF, (R) Erics/ Shutterstock; 89 Daxiao Productions/Shutterstock; 90 (B) Everett Collection/Shutterstock, (C) KittyVector/Shutterstock; 91 Komkrit Noenpoempisut/Shutterstock; 92 (TCL) Africa Studio/Shutterstock, (BCL) Petrenko Andriy/Shutterstock, (BCR) Deep OV/Shutterstock, (BL) Low Sugar/Shutterstock, (BR) Oleksandr Grechin/Shutterstock, (TCR) Dushlik/Shutterstock, (TL) Room27/Shutterstock, (TR) Diane Picard/Shutterstock; 93 (BL) Monkey Business Images/Shutterstock, (BR) Dolgachov/123RF, (TL) Pressmaster/Shutterstock, (TR) Rob Marmion/Shutterstock; 94 (B) Michaeljung/Shutterstock, (C) Diane Picard/Shutterstock, (T) Dushlik/Shutterstock; 95 (BL) Eric Isselee/ Shutterstock, (BR) Shutterstock, (C) Eric Isselee/Shutterstock, (CL) Pandapaw/Shutterstock, (CR) Xpixel/Shutterstock, (TL) Isselee/123RF, (TR) Smit/Shutterstock; 96 (TR) Anton Starikov/123RF,

(BC) Alhovik/Shutterstock, (BL) Fotomaster/Fotolia, (BR) Phant/Shutterstock, (C) Ivan Smuk/Shutterstock, (CL) Michaeljung/Shutterstock, (CR) Topseller/Shutterstock, (TC) Igor Terekhov/123RF, (TL) Africa Studio/Shutterstock; **98** (B) Monkey Business Images/Shutterstock, (C) Goodluz/Shutterstock, (T) Room27/Shutterstock; **120** Neirfy/123RF; **124** AlohaHawaii/Shutterstock; **128** (Bkgd) John Brueske/Shutterstock, (BL) Donna Beeler/Shutterstock; **129** (L) Jon Helgason/123RF, (R) Chris Willemsen/123RF; **130** (BL) Be Good/Shutterstock, (BCL) Denis Kuvaev/Shutterstock, (TCL) Eric Isselee/Shutterstock, (TL) Phant/Shutterstock; **131** (C) Sataporn Jiwjalaen/123RF, (B) VisanuPhotoshop/Shutterstock, (T) Roblan/123RF; **134** (B) Brocreative/Shutterstock, (C) Darya Petrenko/123RF, (T) VisanuPhotoshop/Shutterstock; **140** (L) Everett Historical/Shutterstock, (R) Castleski/Shutterstock; **143** (Bkgd) Picksell/Shutterstock, (BR) Reg Lancaster/Getty Images; **144** (Bkgd) Fedorov Oleksiy/Shutterstock, (T) Michael Ochs Archives/Getty Images; **145** MixPix/Alamy Stock Photo; **146** Bettmann/Getty Images; **147** CBS Photo Archive/Getty Images; **148** Morton Broffman/Getty Images; **149** Monkey Business Images/Shutterstock; **150** Jupiterimages/Getty Images; **151** Reg Lancaster/Getty Images; **152** (C) MixPix/Alamy Stock Photo, (L) Michael Ochs Archives/Getty Images, (R) Morton Broffman/Getty Images; **160** Reg Lancaster/Getty Images; **164** Wang Tom/123RF; **165** Soloviova Liudmyla/Shutterstock; **166** (B) Africa Studio/Shutterstock, (C) Dragon Images/Shutterstock, (T) Tatiana Popova/Shutterstock; **167** (BCL) Val Thoermer/Shutterstock, (BL) Pavla/Shutterstock, (TCL) Artem Voropai/Shutterstock, (TL) George Rudy/Shutterstock; **170** (BCR) Littlekidmoment/Shutterstock, (BR) Evgeniy Kalinovskiy/Shutterstock, (TCR) Littlekidmoment/Shutterstock, (TR) Igor Kisselev/Shutterstock; **174** (BCL) Syda Productions/Shutterstock, (BL) Baloncici/Shutterstock, (TCL) JaySi/Shutterstock, (TL) Asia Images Group/Shutterstock; **193** (BL) Rawpixel/Shutterstock, (BR) Monticello/Shutterstock, (C) Monkey Business Images/Shutterstock, (CL) Margojh/123RF, (CR) Microgen/Shutterstock; **196** Monkey Business Images/Shutterstock; **198** (T) The Len/Shutterstock, (B) Tratong/Shutterstock; **200** (BR) Performance Image/Alamy Stock Photo, Michael Doolittle/Alamy Stock Photo, Cozy nook/Shutterstock; **201** (TR) Picksell/Shutterstock, Reg Lancaster/Getty Images, (BR) ClassicStock/Alamy Stock Photo; **202** (BCR) Eric Isselee/Shutterstock, (BL) Jurasy/Shutterstock, (TCL) Anatoly Tiplyashin/Shutterstock, (TL) Sergio Schnitzler/Shutterstock; **203** (B) Antonio Gravante/Shutterstock, (C) Apollofoto/Shutterstock, (T) Efanov Aleksey Anatolievich/Shutterstock; **206** (BCR) Bohbeh/Shutterstock, (CR) Paul Orr/Shutterstock, (TCR) F_nitta/Shutterstock, (BR) Rosa Jay/Shutterstock, (TR) Tsekhmister/Shutterstock; **210** (B) Jamie Hooper/Shutterstock, (C) Streika/Shutterstock, (T) ShutterOK/Shutterstock; **211** (BL) Sergio Schnitzler/Shutterstock, (BR) Jurasy/Shutterstock, (CL) Tim Large/Shutterstock, (CR) Design56/Shutterstock, (TL) Alex Staroseltsev/Shutterstock, (TR) R. Gino Santa Maria/Shutterstock; **212** ClassicStock/Alamy Stock Photo; **214** ClassicStock/Alamy Stock Photo; **215** Shotshop GmbH/Alamy Stock Photo; **216** Granata68/Shutterstock; **217** ClassicStock/Alamy Stock Photo; **220** Amenic181/Shutterstock; **221** (BL) Againphoto/Shutterstock, (BR) Marco Brockmann/Shutterstock, (CR) Hemis/Alamy Stock Photo, (TL) Haveseen/Shutterstock, (TR) Emilio100/Shutterstock; **223** (B) Prudencio Alvarez/123RF, (T) Masarik/Shutterstock; **224** (B) Tracey Helmboldt/Shutterstock, (T) Vintage Images/Alamy Stock Photo; **225** (B) DutchScenery/Getty Images, (T) AlohaHawaii/Shutterstock; **226** (B) Masarik/Shutterstock, (T) Openfinal/Shutterstock; **227** Michael Ochs Archives/Getty Images.

Illustrations

21, 23–25 Yu-Mei Han; **29, 67** Tim Johnson; **52–53** René Milot; **57** Laura Zarrin; **59, 61–63** Caroline Hu; **69–77, 80, 86** Lisa Fields; **97, 99–101** Estudio Haus; **105, 141, 177** Ken Bowser; **107–115, 118, 120** Olga Skomorokhova; **133, 135–137** Carlos Aón; **138–139** Marc Monés; **169, 171–173** Linda Prater; **179–188** Teresa Martinez; **205, 207–209** Caroline Hu